THE WORKS OF
EUGENE FIELD

Vol. VI

"Hark you! from yonder Sabine farm
Echo the songs of long ago"

Drawn by August F. Jaccaci

THE WRITINGS IN PROSE AND VERSE OF EUGENE FIELD

ECHOES FROM THE SABINE FARM ❧ ❧ ❧ ❧

CHARLES SCRIBNER'S SONS ❧ NEW YORK ❧ 1896

INTRODUCTION

ONE Sunday evening in the winter of 1890 Eugene Field and the writer were walking in Lake View, Chicago, on their way to visit the library of a common friend, when the subject of publishing a book for Field came up for discussion.

The Little Book of Western Verse and The Little Book of Profitable Tales had been privately printed the year before at Chicago, and Field had been frequently reminded that the writer was ready and willing to stand sponsor for any new volume he, Field, might desire to bring out.

" The only thing I have on hand that might make a book," said Field, "are some few paraphrases of the Odes of Horace which my brother, 'Rose,' and I have been fooling over, and which, truth to tell, are certainly freely rendered. There are not enough of them, but we 'll do some more, and I 'll add a brief Life of Horace as a preface or introduction."

It is to be regretted that Field never carried out his intention with respect to this last, for he had given much thought and study to the great Roman satirist, and what Eugene Field could have said upon the subject must have been of interest. It is my belief that as he thought upon the matter it grew too great for him to handle within the space he had at first determined, and that tucked away within the recesses of his literary intentions was the determination, nullified by his early death, to write, *con amore,* a life of Quintus Horatius Flaccus.

This determination to write separately an extended account of Horace greatly reduced the bulk of the material intended for the Sabine Echoes, and it was with respect to this that Field apologetically and, as was his wont, humorously wrote:

"The volume may be rather thin *in corpore,* but think how hefty it will be intellectually."

When it came to the discussion of how

many copies should be printed it was suggested that the edition be an exceedingly limited one, in order to cause as much scrambling and heartburning as possible among our bibliophilic brethren. And never shall I forget the seriousness of the man's face, nor the roars of laughter that followed, when he suggested that fifty copies only should be made, and that we should reserve one each and burn the other forty-eight!

It was a biting cold night and we had been loitering by the way, stopping to debate each point as it arose — but now we plunged on with excess of motion to keep ourselves warm, breaking out with occasional peals of laughter as we thought of our plan to make the publication what the booksellers call " excessively rare."

Field, elsewhere, has said he did not know why the original intention as to the destruction of the forty-eight copies was not carried out, but the answer is not far away. As the time for publication approached it was found impossible that such and such a friend should be forgotten in the matter of a copy, and so it went on until it was deemed prudent to add fifty to the number originally intended to be issued, and that decision, in the light of what followed, proved to be an eminently wise one.   More than once some to me unknown friend of Field would write a pleasant lie as a reason to gain possession of the book, and up in a corner of the letter would be found an endorsement of the request after this fashion:

What 's writ below
I 'd have you know
Nor falsehood nor romance is ;
It 's solemn truth,
So grant the youth
The boon he seeks, dear Francis.
EUGENE FIELD.

It is perhaps unnecessary to add that, however flimsy the pretext upon which the request for a copy was made, it never failed of its object if it brought with it Field's endorsement.   Among many pleasant utterances on this subject Field has said that but for the writer the Horatian verses would not have been given to the world — and this has been taken to mean more than was intended, and much unearned praise has been bestowed. But, in allusion to the original issue of the Odes, Field added, "in this charming guise," which places quite another construction upon the matter.

It may be that the enthusiasm displayed not only pleased Field, and incited him and his brother Roswell to perform that which, otherwise, might have been indefinitely deferred, but there is no question but that they intended to publish the Horatian odes at some time or another. Field was greatly delighted with the reception of this work, and I once heard him say it would outlive all his other books. He came naturally by his love of the classics. His father was a splendid scholar who obliged his sons to correspond with him in Latin. Field's favorite ode was the Bandusian Spring, the paraphrasing of which in the styles of the various writers of different periods gave him genuine joy and is perhaps the choice bit of the collection. The Echoes from the Sabine Farm was the most ambitious work Field had attempted up to the time of its issue. He was not at all sure that the

public for whom he wrote, what following
he then felt was his own, would accept his
efforts in this direction with any sort of ac-
claim. Unquestionably, Field, at all times,
believed in himself and in his power ulti-
mately to make a name, as every man must
who achieves success, but he was as far
from believing that the public would accept
him as an interpreter of Horatian odes as
was Edward Fitzgerald with respect to
Omar Khayyám. In short, he looked upon
his work in the original publication of Echoes
from the Sabine Farm as a labor of love—
an effort from which some reputation might
come, but certainly no monetary remunera-
tion. It was because he so regarded it that
he permitted the work to be first issued un-
der the bolstering influence of a patron. It
was, so he thought, an excellent opportu-
nity to show his friends and acquaintances
that his Pegasus was capable of soaring to
classic heights, and he little dreamed that
the paraphrasing of the Odes of Horace over
which "Rose and I have been fooling"
would be required for a *popular* edition.
With the announcement of the Scribner edi-

tion of The Sabine Echoes came also the intelligence of Field's death.

I have found people who were somewhat puzzled as to the exact intentions of the Fields with respect to these translations and paraphrases. However, there can be no chance for mistake even to the veriest embryonic reader of Horace, if he will but remember that, while some of these transcriptions are indeed very faithful reproductions or adaptations of the original, others again are to be accepted as the very riot of burlesque verse-making.

The last stanza in the epilogue of this book reads:

> Or if we part to meet no more
> This side the misty Stygian river,
> Be sure of this: On yonder shore
> Sweet cheer awaiteth such as we —
> A Sabine pagan's heaven, O friend —
> And fellowship that knows no end.

FRANCIS WILSON.

January 22, 1896.

TO M. L. GRAY.

Come, dear old friend, and with us twain
    To calm Digentian groves repair;
The turtle coos his sweet refrain
    And posies are a-blooming there;
And there the romping Sabine girls
Bind myrtle in their lustrous curls.

I know a certain ilex-tree
    Whence leaps a fountain cool and clear.
Its voices summon you and me;
    Come, let us haste to share its cheer!
Methinks the rapturous song it sings
Should woo our thoughts from mortal things.

But, good old friend, I charge thee well,
    Watch thou my brother all the while,
Lest some fair Lydia cast her spell
    Round him unschooled in female guile.
Those damsels have no charms for me;
Guard thou that brother,—I'll guard thee!

xiii

And, lo, sweet friend! behold this cup,
    Round which the garlands intertwine;
With Massic it is foaming up,
    And we would drink to thee and thine.
And of the draught thou shalt partake,
Who lov'st us for our father's sake.

Hark you! from yonder Sabine farm
    Echo the songs of long ago,
With power to soothe and grace to charm
    What ills humanity may know;
With that sweet music in the air,
'T is Love and Summer everywhere.

So, though no grief consumes our lot
    (Since all our lives have been discreet),
Come, in this consecrated spot,
    Let 's see if pagan cheer be sweet.
Now, then, the songs; but, first, more wine.
The gods be with you, friends of mine!

                                        E. F.

The Contents of this Book

xv

CONTENTS

CONTENTS

Echoes from the Sabine Farm

AN INVITATION TO MÆCENAS

DEAR, noble friend! a virgin cask
  Of wine solicits your attention;
  And roses fair, to deck your hair,
 And things too numerous to mention.
So tear yourself awhile away
 From urban turmoil, pride, and splendor,
And deign to share what humble fare
 And sumptuous fellowship I tender.
The sweet content retirement brings
Smoothes out the ruffled front of kings.

The evil planets have combined
 To make the weather hot and hotter;
By parboiled streams the shepherd dreams
 Vainly of ice-cream soda-water.

And meanwhile you, defying heat,
   With patriotic ardor ponder
On what old Rome essays at home,
   And what her heathen do out yonder.
Mæcenas, no such vain alarm
Disturbs the quiet of this farm!

God in His providence obscures
   The goal beyond this vale of sorrow,
And smiles at men in pity when
   They seek to penetrate the morrow.
With faith that all is for the best,
   Let 's bear what burdens are presented,
That we shall say, let come what may,
   " We die, as we have lived, contented!
Ours is to-day; God's is the rest,—
He doth ordain who knoweth best."

Dame Fortune plays me many a prank.
   When she is kind, oh, how I go it!
But if again she 's harsh,— why, then
   I am a very proper poet!

When favoring gales bring in my ships,
    I hie to Rome and live in clover;
Elsewise I steer my skiff out here,
    And anchor till the storm blows over.
Compulsory virtue is the charm
Of life upon the Sabine farm!

CHLORIS PROPERLY REBUKED

CHLORIS, my friend, I pray you your
misconduct to forswear;
The wife of poor old Ibycus should have
more *savoir faire.*
A woman at your time of life, and drawing
near death's door,
Should not play with the girly girls, and
think she's *en rapport.*

What's good enough for Pholoe you cannot
well essay;
Your daughter very properly courts the *jeu-
nesse dorée,*—
A Thyiad, who, when timbrel beats, cannot
her joy restrain,
But plays the kid, and laughs and giggles
à l'Américaine.

'T is more becoming, Madame, in a creature
    old and poor,
To sit and spin than to engage in an *affaire
    d'amour.*
The lutes, the roses, and the wine drained
    deep are not for you;
Remember what the poet says: *Ce monde
    est plein de fous!*

TO THE FOUNTAIN OF BANDUSIA

O FOUNTAIN of Bandusia!
  Whence crystal waters flow,
With garlands gay and wine I 'll pay
  The sacrifice I owe;
A sportive kid with budding horns
  I have, whose crimson blood
Anon shall dye and sanctify
  Thy cool and babbling flood.

O fountain of Bandusia!
  The Dog-star's hateful spell
No evil brings into the springs
  That from thy bosom well;
Here oxen, wearied by the plow,
  The roving cattle here
Hasten in quest of certain rest,
  And quaff thy gracious cheer.

O fountain of Bandusia!
  Ennobled shalt thou be,
For I shall sing the joys that spring
  Beneath yon ilex-tree.
Yes, fountain of Bandusia,
  Posterity shall know
The cooling brooks that from thy nooks
  Singing and dancing go.

TO THE FOUNTAIN OF BANDUSIA

O FOUNTAIN of Bandusia ! more glit-
tering than glass,
And worthy of the pleasant wine and toasts
that freely pass;
More worthy of the flowers with which
thou modestly art hid,
To-morrow willing hands shall sacrifice to
thee a kid.

In vain the glory of the brow where proudly
swell above
The growing horns, significant of battle and
of love;
For in thy honor he shall die,— the offspring
of the herd,—
And with his crimson life-blood thy cold
waters shall be stirred.

The Dog-star's cruel season, with its fierce
and blazing heat,
Has never sent its scorching rays into thy
glad retreat;
The oxen, wearied with the plow, the herd
which wanders near,
Have found a grateful respite and delicious
coolness here.

When of the graceful ilex on the hollow
rocks I sing,
Thou shalt become illustrious, O sweet Bandusian spring!
Among the noble fountains which have been
enshrined in fame,
Thy dancing, babbling waters shall in song
our homage claim.

THE PREFERENCE DECLARED

BOY, I detest the Persian pomp;
   I hate those linden-bark devices;
And as for roses, holy Moses!
   They can't be got at living prices!
Myrtle is good enough for us,—
   For *you,* as bearer of my flagon ;
For *me,* supine beneath this vine,
   Doing my best to get a jag on!

A TARDY APOLOGY

I

Mᴀ̃CENAS, you will be my death,—
    though friendly you profess yourself,—
If to me in a strain like this so often you ad-
    dress yourself :
"Come, Holly, why this laziness ? Why
    indolently shock you us ?
Why with Lethean cups fall into desuetude
    innocuous ? "

A god, Mæcenas! yea, a god hath proved
    the very curse of me !
If my iambics are not done, pray, do not
    think the worse of me;
Anacreon for young Bathyllus burned with-
    out apology,
And wept his simple measures on a sample
    of conchology.

Now, you yourself, Mæcenas, are enjoying
    this beatitude;
If by no brighter beauty Ilium fell, you 've
    cause for gratitude.
A certain Phryne keeps me on the rack with
    lovers numerous;
This is the artful hussy's neat conception of
    the humorous!

A TARDY APOLOGY

II

YOU ask me, friend,
    Why I don't send
The long since due-and-paid-for numbers;
    Why, songless, I
    As drunken lie
Abandoned to Lethean slumbers.

    Long time ago
    (As well you know)
I started in upon that carmen;
    My work was vain,—
    But why complain?
When gods forbid, how helpless are men!

Some ages back,
The sage Anack
Courted a frisky Samian body,
Singing her praise
In metered phrase
As flowing as his bowls of toddy.

Till I was hoarse
Might I discourse
Upon the cruelties of Venus;
'T were waste of time
As well of rhyme,
For you 've been there yourself, Mæcenas!

Perfect your bliss
If some fair miss
Love you yourself and *not* your minæ;
I, fortune's sport,
All vainly court
The beauteous, polyandrous Phryne!

TO THE SHIP OF STATE

O SHIP of state,
Shall new winds bear you back upon
the sea?
What are you doing? Seek the harbor's lee
Ere 't is too late!

Do you bemoan
Your side was stripped of oarage in the
blast?
Swift Africus has weakened, too, your
mast;
The sailyards groan.

17

Of cables bare,
Your keel can scarce endure the lordly wave.
Your sails are rent; you have no gods to
  save,
        Or answer pray'r.

        Though Pontic pine,
The noble daughter of a far-famed wood,
You boast your lineage and title good,—
        A useless line!

        The sailor there
In painted sterns no reassurance finds;
Unless you owe derision to the winds,
        Beware — beware!

        My grief erewhile,
But now my care — my longing! shun the
  seas
That flow between the gleaming Cyclades,
        Each shining isle.

QUITTING AGAIN

THE hero of
   Affairs of love
By far too numerous to be mentioned,
    And scarred as I 'm,
    It seemeth time
That I were mustered out and pensioned.

    So on this wall
    My lute and all
I hang, and dedicate to Venus;
    And I implore
    But one thing more
Ere all is at an end between us.

O goddess fair
Who reignest where
The weather 's seldom bleak and snowy,
This boon I urge:
In anger scourge
My old cantankerous sweetheart, Chloe!

SAILOR AND SHADE

SAILOR

YOU, who have compassed land and sea,
  Now all unburied lie;
All vain your store of human lore,
  For you were doomed to die.
The sire of Pelops likewise fell,—
  Jove's honored mortal guest;
So king and sage of every age
  At last lie down to rest.
Plutonian shades enfold the ghost
  Of that majestic one
Who taught as truth that he, forsooth,
  Had once been Pentheus' son;
Believe who may, he 's passed away,
  And what he did is done.
A last night comes alike to all;
  One path we all must tread,

Through sore disease or stormy seas
   Or fields with corpses red.
Whate'er our deeds, that pathway leads
   To regions of the dead.

SHADE

The fickle twin Illyrian gales
   O'erwhelmed me on the wave;
But you that live, I pray you give
   My bleaching bones a grave!
Oh, then when cruel tempests rage
   You all unharmed shall be;
Jove's mighty hand shall guard by land
   And Neptune's on the sea.
Perchance you fear to do what may
   Bring evil to your race?
Oh, rather fear that like me here
   You 'll lack a burial place.
So, though you be in proper haste,
   Bide long enough, I pray,
To give me, friend, what boon shall send
   My soul upon its way!

LET US HAVE PEACE

IN maudlin spite let Thracians fight
    Above their bowls of liquor;
But such as we, when on a spree,
    Should never brawl and bicker!

These angry words and clashing swords
    Are quite *de trop,* I 'm thinking;
Brace up, my boys, and hush your noise,
    And drown your wrath in drinking.

Aha, 't is fine, — this mellow wine
    With which our host would dope us!
Now let us hear what pretty dear
    Entangles him of Opus.

I see you blush,—nay, comrades, hush!
　Come, friend, though they despise you,
Tell me the name of that fair dame,—
　Perchance I may advise you.

O wretched youth! and is it truth
　You love that fickle lady?
I, doting dunce, courted her once;
　Since when, she 's reckoned shady!

TO QUINTUS DELLIUS

BE tranquil, Dellius, I pray;
 For though you pine your life away
  With dull complaining breath,
Or speed with song and wine each day,
  Still, still your doom is death.

Where the white poplar and the pine
In glorious arching shade combine,
  And the brook singing goes,
Bid them bring store of nard and wine
  And garlands of the rose.

Let 's live while chance and youth obtain;
Soon shall you quit this fair domain
  Kissed by the Tiber's gold,
And all your earthly pride and gain
  Some heedless heir shall hold.

One ghostly boat shall some time bear
From scenes of mirthfulness or care
    Each fated human soul,—
Shall waft and leave its burden where
    The waves of Lethe roll.

So come, I prithee, Dellius mine;
Let 's sing our songs and drink our wine
    In that sequestered nook
Where the white poplar and the pine
    Stand listening to the brook.

POKING FUN AT XANTHIAS

O F your love for your handmaid you
     need feel no shame.
  Don't apologize, Xanthias, pray;
Remember, Achilles the proud felt a flame
  For Brissy, his slave, as they say.
Old Telamon's son, fiery Ajax, was moved
  By the captive Tecmessa's ripe charms;
And Atrides, suspending the feast, it be-
  hooved
  To gather a girl to his arms.

Now, how do you know that this yellow-
  haired maid
  (This Phyllis you fain would enjoy)

Has n't parents whose wealth would cast
    you in the shade,—
  Who would ornament you, Xan, my
      boy?
Very likely the poor chick sheds copious
    tears,
  And is bitterly thinking the while
Of the royal good times of her earlier years,
  When her folks regulated the style!

It won't do at all, my dear boy, to believe
  That she of whose charms you are proud
Is beautiful only as means to deceive,—
  Merely one of the horrible crowd.
So constant a sweetheart, so loving a wife,
  So averse to all notions of greed
Was surely not born of a mother whose life
  Is a chapter you 'd better not read.

As an unbiased party I feel it my place
  (For I don't like to do things by halves)

To compliment Phyllis,— her arms and her
    face
  And (excuse me!) her delicate calves.
Tut, tut! don't get angry, my boy, or
    suspect
  You have any occasion to fear
A man whose deportment is always correct,
  And is now in his forty-first year!

TO ARISTIUS FUSCUS

FUSCUS, whoso to good inclines,
  And is a faultless liver,
Nor Moorish spear nor bow need fear,
  Nor poison-arrowed quiver.

Ay, though through desert wastes he roam,
  Or scale the rugged mountains,
Or rest beside the murmuring tide
  Of weird Hydaspan fountains!

Lo, on a time, I gayly paced
  The Sabine confines shady,
And sung in glee of Lalage,
  My own and dearest lady;

And as I sung, a monster wolf
   Slunk through the thicket from me;
But for that song, as I strolled along,
   He would have overcome me!

Set me amid those poison mists
   Which no fair gale dispelleth,
Or in the plains where silence reigns,
   And no thing human dwelleth,—

Still shall I love my Lalage,
   Still sing her tender graces;
And while I sing, my theme shall bring
   Heaven to those desert places!

TO ALBIUS TIBULLUS

I

NOT to lament that rival flame
    Wherewith the heartless Glycera
  scorns you,
Nor waste your time in maudlin rhyme,
    How many a modern instance warns you!

Fair-browed Lycoris pines away
    Because her Cyrus loves another;
The ruthless churl informs the girl
    He loves her only as a brother!

For he, in turn, courts Pholoe,—
    A maid unscotched of love's fierce virus;
Why, goats will mate with wolves they
      hate
    Ere Pholoe will mate with Cyrus!

Ah, weak and hapless human hearts,
  By cruel Mother Venus fated
To spend this life in hopeless strife,
  Because incongruously mated!

Such torture, Albius, is my lot;
  For, though a better mistress wooed me,
My Myrtale has captured me,
  And with her cruelties subdued me!

TO ALBIUS TIBULLUS

II

GRIEVE not, my Albius, if thoughts of
Glycera may haunt you,
Nor chant your mournful elegies because
she faithless proves;
If now a younger man than you this cruel
charmer loves,
Let not the kindly favors of the past rise up
to taunt you.

Lycoris of the little brow for Cyrus feels a
passion,
And Cyrus, on the other hand, toward
Pholoe inclines;
But ere this crafty Cyrus can accomplish
his designs
She-goats will wed Apulian wolves in defer-
ence to fashion.

Such is the will, the cruel will, of love-in-
    citing Venus,
    Who takes delight in wanton sport and
    ill-considered jokes,
    And brings ridiculous misfits beneath her
    brazen yokes,—
A very infelicitous proceeding, just between
    us.

As for myself, young Myrtale, slave-born
    and lacking graces,
    And wilder than the Adrian tides which
    form Calabrian bays,
    Entangled me in pleasing chains and com-
    promising ways,
When — just my luck — a better girl was
    courting my embraces.

TO MÆCENAS

MÆCENAS, thou of royalty's descent,
Both my protector and dear ornament,
Among humanity's conditions are
Those who take pleasure in the flying car,
Whirling Olympian dust, as on they roll,
And shunning with the glowing wheel the
    goal;
While the ennobling palm, the prize of worth,
Exalts them to the gods, the lords of earth.

Here one is happy if the fickle crowd
His name the threefold honor has allowed;
And there another, if into his stores
Comes what is swept from Libyan threshing-
    floors.
He who delights to till his father's lands,
And grasps the delving-hoe with willing
    hands,

Can never to Attalic offers hark,
Or cut the Myrtoan Sea with Cyprian bark.
The merchant, timorous of Afric's breeze,
When fiercely struggling with Icarian seas
Praises the restful quiet of his home,
Nor wishes from the peaceful fields to roam;
Ah, speedily his shattered ships he mends,—
To poverty his lesson ne'er extends.

One there may be who never scorns to fill
His cups with mellow draughts from Massic's
    hill,
Nor from the busy day an hour to wean,
Now stretched at length beneath the arbute
    green,
Now at the softly whispering spring, to
    dream
Of the fair nymphs who haunt the sacred
    stream.
For camp and trump and clarion some have
    zest,—
The cruel wars the mothers so detest.

'Neath the cold sky the hunter spends his
    life,
Unmindful of his home and tender wife,
Whether the doe is seen by faithful hounds
Or Marsian boar through the fine meshes
    bounds.

But as for me, the ivy-wreaths, the prize
Of learned brows, exalt me to the skies;
The shady grove, the nymphs and satyrs
    there,
Draw me away from people everywhere;
If it may be, Euterpe's flute inspires,
Or Polyhymnia strikes the Lesbian lyres;
And if you place me where no bard debars,
With head exalted I shall strike the stars!

TO HIS BOOK

YOU vain, self-conscious little book,
    Companion of my happy days,
How eagerly you seem to look
For wider fields to spread your lays;
    My desk and locks cannot contain you,
    Nor blush of modesty restrain you.

    Well, then, begone, fool that thou art!
But do not come to me and cry,
    When critics strike you to the heart:
"Oh, wretched little book am I!"
    You know I tried to educate you
    To shun the fate that must await you.

39

In youth you may encounter friends
(Pray this prediction be not wrong),
　But wait until old age descends
And thumbs have smeared your gentlest
　　　song;
　　Then will the moths connive to eat you
　　And rural libraries secrete you.

　However, should a friend some word
Of my obscure career request,
　Tell him how deeply I was stirred
To spread my wings beyond the nest;
　　Take from my years, which are before you,
　　To boom my merits, I implore you.

　Tell him that I am short and fat,
Quick in my temper, soon appeased,
　　With locks of gray, — but what of that?
Loving the sun, with nature pleased.
　　I 'm more than four and forty, hark you, —
　　But ready for a night off, mark you!

40

FAME *vs.* RICHES

THE Greeks had genius,— 't was a gift
    The Muse vouchsafed in glorious
    measure;
The boon of Fame they made their aim
    And prized above all worldly treasure.

But *we,*— how do we train *our* youth?
    Not in the arts that are immortal,
But in the greed for gains that speed
    From him who stands at Death's dark
    portal.

Ah, when this slavish love of gold
    Once binds the soul in greasy fetters,
How prostrate lies,— how droops and dies
    The great, the noble cause of letters!

THE LYRIC MUSE

I LOVE the lyric muse!
  For when mankind ran wild in grooves
 Came holy Orpheus with his songs
And turned men's hearts from bestial loves,
  From brutal force and savage wrongs;
Amphion, too, and on his lyre
  Made such sweet music all the day
That rocks, instinct with warm desire,
  Pursued him in his glorious way.

 I love the lyric muse!
Hers was the wisdom that of yore
  Taught man the rights of fellow man,
Taught him to worship God the more,
  And to revere love's holy ban.

Hers was the hand that jotted down
  The laws correcting divers wrongs;
And so came honor and renown
  To bards and to their noble songs.

I love the lyric muse!
Old Homer sung unto the lyre;
  Tyrtæus, too, in ancient days;
Still warmed by their immortal fire,
  How doth our patriot spirit blaze!
The oracle, when questioned, sings;
  So our first steps in life are taught.
In verse we soothe the pride of kings,
  In verse the drama has been wrought.

I love the lyric muse!
Be not ashamed, O noble friend,
  In honest gratitude to pay
Thy homage to the gods that send
  This boon to charm all ill away.

43

With solemn tenderness revere
This voiceful glory as a shrine
Wherein the quickened heart may hear
The counsels of a voice divine!

A COUNTERBLAST AGAINST GARLIC

MAY the man who has cruelly murdered
    his sire —
    A crime to be punished with death —
Be condemned to eat garlic till he shall expire
    Of his own foul and venomous breath !
What stomachs these rustics must have who
        can eat
    This dish that Canidia made,
Which imparts to my colon a torturous heat,
    And a poisonous look, I 'm afraid!

They say that ere Jason attempted to yoke
    The fire-breathing bulls to the plow
He smeared his whole body with garlic, — a
        joke
    Which I fully appreciate now.

45

When Medea gave Glauce her beautiful
    dress,
  In which garlic was scattered about,
It was cruel and rather low-down, I confess,
  But it settled the point beyond doubt.

On thirsty Apulia ne'er has the sun
  Inflicted such terrible heat;
As for Hercules' robe, although poisoned,
    't was fun
  When compared with this garlic we eat!
Mæcenas, if ever on garbage like this
  You express a desire to be fed,
May Mrs. Mæcenas object to your kiss,
  And lie at the foot of the bed!

AN EXCUSE FOR LALAGE

To bear the yoke not yet your love's
    submissive neck is bent,
To share a husband's toil, or grasp his amor-
    ous intent;
Over the fields, in cooling streams, the heifer
    longs to go,
Now with the calves disporting where the
    pussy-willows grow.

Give up your thirst for unripe grapes, and,
    trust me, you shall learn
How quickly in the autumn time to purple
    they will turn.
Soon she will follow you, for age steals
    swiftly on the maid;
And all the precious years that you have
    lost she will have paid.

Soon she will seek a lord, beloved as Pholoe,
    the coy,
Or Chloris, or young Gyges, that deceitful,
    girlish boy,
Whom, if you placed among the girls, and
    loosed his flowing locks,
The wondering guests could not decide
    which one decorum shocks.

AN APPEAL TO LYCE

LYCE, the gods have heard my prayers,
    as gods will hear the dutiful,
And brought old age upon you, though you
    still affect the beautiful.
You sport among the boys, and drink and
    chatter on quite aimlessly;
And in your cups with quavering voice you
    torment Cupid shamelessly.

For blooming Chia, Cupid has a feeling more
    than brotherly;
He knows a handsaw from a hawk when-
    ever winds are southerly.
He pats her pretty cheeks, but looks on you
    as a monstrosity;
Your wrinkles and your yellow teeth excite
    his animosity.

For jewels bright and purple Coan robes
    you are not dressable;
Unhappily for you, the public records are
    accessible.
Where is your charm, and where your bloom
    and gait so firm and sensible,
That drew my love from Cinara,— a lapse
    most indefensible ?

To my poor Cinara in youth Death came
    with great celerity;
Egad, that never can be said of you with
    any verity!
The old crow that you are, the teasing boys
    will jeer, compelling you
To roost at home.   Reflect, all this is straight
    that I am telling you.

A ROMAN WINTER-PIECE

I

SEE, Thaliarch mine, how, white with
   snow,
  Soracte mocks the sullen sky;
How, groaning loud, the woods are bowed,
  And chained with frost the rivers lie.

Pile, pile the logs upon the hearth;
  We 'll melt away the envious cold:
And, better yet, sweet friend, we 'll wet
  Our whistles with some four-year-old.

Commit all else unto the gods,
  Who, when it pleaseth them, shall bring
To fretful deeps and wooded steeps
  The mild, persuasive grace of Spring.

Let not To-morrow, but To-day,
   Your ever active thoughts engage;
Frisk, dance, and sing, and have your fling,
   Unharmed, unawed of crabbed Age.

Let 's steal content from Winter's wrath,
   And glory in the artful theft,
That years from now folks shall allow
   'T was cold indeed when we got left.

So where the whisperings and the mirth
   Of girls invite a sportive chap,
Let 's fare awhile,— aha, you smile;
   You guess my meaning,— *verbum sap.*

A ROMAN WINTER-PIECE

II

NOW stands Soracte white with snow,
    now bend the laboring trees,
And with the sharpness of the frost the stag-
    nant rivers freeze.
Pile up the billets on the hearth, to warmer
    cheer incline,
And draw, my Thaliarchus, from the Sabine
    jar the wine.

The rest leave to the gods, who still the
    fiercely warring wind,
And to the morrow's store of good or evil
    give no mind.
Whatever day your fortune grants, that day
    mark up for gain;
And in your youthful bloom do not the sweet
    amours disdain.

Now on the Campus and the squares, when
    evening shades descend,
Soft whisperings again are heard, and loving
    voices blend;
And now the low delightful laugh betrays
    the lurking maid,
While from her slowly yielding arms the
    forfeiture is paid.

TO DIANA

O VIRGIN, tri-formed goddess fair,
    The guardian of the groves and hills,
Who hears the girls in their despair
   Cry out in childbirth's cruel ills,
     And saves them from the Stygian flow!
Let the pine-tree my cottage near
   Be sacred to thee evermore,
That I may give to it each year
   With joy the life-blood of the boar,
     Now thinking of the sidelong blow.

TO HIS LUTE

IF ever in the sylvan shade
  A song immortal we have made,
Come now, O lute, I prithee come,
Inspire a song of Latium!

A Lesbian first thy glories proved;
In arms and in repose he loved
To sweep thy dulcet strings, and raise
His voice in Love's and Liber's praise.
The Muses, too, and him who clings
To Mother Venus' apron-strings,
And Lycus beautiful, he sung
In those old days when you were young.

O shell, that art the ornament
Of Phœbus, bringing sweet content
To Jove, and soothing troubles all,—
Come and requite me, when I call!

TO LEUCONÖE

I

WHAT end the gods may have or-
dained for me,
And what for thee,
   Seek not to learn, Leuconöe; we may not
      know.
Chaldean tables cannot bring us rest.
'T is for the best
   To bear in patience what may come, or
      weal or woe.

If for more winters our poor lot is cast,
Or this the last,
   Which on the crumbling rocks has dashed
      Etruscan seas,

Strain clear the wine; this life is short, at best.
Take hope with zest,
    And, trusting not To-morrow, snatch To-
        day for ease!

TO LEUCONÖE

II

SEEK not, Leuconöe, to know how long
   you 're going to live yet,
What boons the gods will yet withhold, or
   what they 're going to give yet;
For Jupiter will have his way, despite how
   much we worry,—
Some will hang on for many a day, and some
   die in a hurry.
The wisest thing for you to do is to embark
   this diem
Upon a merry escapade with some such
   bard as I am.
And while we sport I 'll reel you off such
   odes as shall surprise ye;
To-morrow, when the headache comes,—
   well, then I 'll satirize ye!

TO LIGURINUS

I

THOUGH mighty in Love's favor still,
  Though cruel yet, my boy,
When the unwelcome dawn shall chill
    Your pride and youthful joy,
The hair which round your shoulder grows
    Is rudely cut away,
Your color, redder than the rose,
    Is changed by youth's decay,—

Then, Ligurinus, in the glass
    Another you will spy.
And as the shaggy face, alas!
    You see, your grief will cry:
"Why in my youth could I not learn
    The wisdom men enjoy?
Or why to men cannot return
    The smooth cheeks of the boy?"

TO LIGURINUS

II

O CRUEL fair,
  Whose flowing hair
The envy and the pride of all is,
  As onward roll
  The years, that poll
Will get as bald as a billiard ball is;
Then shall your skin, now pink and dimply,
Be tanned to parchment, sear and pimply!

  When you behold
  Yourself grown old,
These words shall speak your spirits
  moody:

" Unhappy one!
What heaps of fun
I 've missed by being goody-goody!
Oh, that I might have felt the hunger
Of loveless age when I was younger!"

THE HAPPY ISLES

OH, come with me to the Happy Isles
    In the golden haze off yonder,
Where the song of the sun-kissed breeze
    beguiles
    And the ocean loves to wander.

Fragrant the vines that mantle those hills,
    Proudly the fig rejoices,
Merrily dance the virgin rills,
    Blending their myriad voices.

Our herds shall suffer no evil there,
    But peacefully feed and rest them;
Never thereto shall prowling bear
    Or serpent come to molest them.

64

Neither shall Eurus, wanton bold,
   Nor feverish drought distress us,
But he that compasseth heat and cold
   Shall temper them both to bless us.

There no vandal foot has trod,
   And the pirate hordes that wander
Shall never profane the sacred sod
   Of those beautiful isles out yonder.

Never a spell shall blight our vines,
   Nor Sirius blaze above us,
But you and I shall drink our wines
   And sing to the loved that love us.

So come with me where Fortune smiles
   And the gods invite devotion,—
Oh, come with me to the Happy Isles
   In the haze of that far-off ocean!

CONSISTENCY

S HOULD painter attach to a fair human
head
  The thick, turgid neck of a stallion,
Or depict a spruce lass with the tail of a
bass,
  I am sure you would guy the rapscallion.

Believe me, dear Pisos, that just such a
freak
  Is the crude and preposterous poem
Which merely abounds in a torrent of
sounds,
  With no depth of reason below 'em.

66

'T is all very well to give license to art,—
  The wisdom of license defend I;
But the line should be drawn at the fripper-
    ish spawn
  Of a mere *cacoethes scribendi.*

It is too much the fashion to strain at ef-
    fects,—
  Yes, that 's what 's the matter with Han-
    nah!
Our popular taste, by the tyros debased,
  Paints each barnyard a grove of Diana!

Should a patron require you to paint a ma-
    rine,
  Would you work in some trees with their
    barks on?
When his strict orders are for a Japanese jar,
  Would you give him a pitcher like Clark-
    son?

67

Now, this is my moral: Compose what you
    may,
  And Fame will be ever far distant
Unless you combine with a simple design
  A treatment in toto consistent.

TO POSTUMUS

O POSTUMUS, my Postumus, the years
    are gliding past,
And piety will never check the wrinkles
    coming fast,
The ravages of time old age's swift advance
    has made,
And death, which unimpeded comes to bear
    us to the shade.

Old friend, although the tearless Pluto you
    may strive to please,
And seek each year with thrice one hundred
    bullocks to appease,
Who keeps the thrice-huge Geryon and
    Tityus his slaves,
Imprisoned fast forevermore with cold and
    sombre waves,

Yet must that flood so terrible be sailed by
    mortals all;
Whether perchance we may be kings and
    live in royal hall,
Or lowly peasants struggling long with pov-
    erty and dearth,
Still must we cross who live upon the favors
    of the earth.

And all in vain from bloody war and contest
    we are free,
And from the waves that hoarsely break
    upon the Adrian Sea;
For our frail bodies all in vain our helpless
    terror grows
In gloomy autumn seasons, when the bane-
    ful south wind blows.

Alas! the black Cocytus, wandering to the
    world below,
That languid river to behold we of this earth
    must go;

To see the grim Danaides, that miserable
race,
And Sisyphus of Æolus, condemned to end-
less chase.

Behind you must you leave your home and
land and wife so dear,
And of the trees, except the hated cypresses,
you rear,
And which around the funeral piles as signs
of mourning grow,
Not one will follow you, their short-lived
master, there below.

Your worthier heir the precious Cæcuban
shall drink galore,
Now with a hundred keys preserved and
guarded in your store,
And stain the pavements, pouring out in
waste the nectar proud,
Better than that with which the pontiffs'
feasts have been endowed.

TO MISTRESS PYRRHA

I

WHAT perfumed, posie-dizened sirrah,
　　With smiles for diet,
Clasps you, O fair but faithless Pyrrha,
　　On the quiet?
For whom do you bind up your tresses,
　　As spun-gold yellow,—
Meshes that go with your caresses,
　　To snare a fellow?

How will he rail at fate capricious,
　　And curse you duly,
Yet now he deems your wiles delicious,—
　　You perfect, truly!
Pyrrha, your love 's a treacherous ocean;
　　He 'll soon fall in there!
Then shall I gloat on his commotion,
　　For *I* have been there!

72

TO MISTRESS PYRRHA

II

WHAT dainty boy with sweet per-
fumes bedewed
Has lavished kisses, Pyrrha, in the cave?
For whom amid the roses, many-hued,
Do you bind back your tresses' yellow wave?

How oft will he deplore your fickle whim,
And wonder at the storm and roughening
deeps,
Who now enjoys you, all in all to him,
And dreams of you, whose only thoughts
he keeps.

73

Wretched are they to whom you seem so
    fair;—
That I escaped the storms, the gods be
    praised!
My dripping garments, offered with a prayer,
Stand as a tablet to the sea-god raised.

TO MELPOMENE

LOFTY and enduring is the monument I 've
    reared:
  Come, tempests, with your bitterness as-
    sailing;
And thou, corrosive blasts of time, by all
    things mortal feared,
  Thy buffets and thy rage are unavailing!

I shall not altogether die: by far my greater
    part
  Shall mock man's common fate in realms
    infernal;
My works shall live as tributes to my genius
    and my art,—
  My works shall be my monument eternal!

While this great Roman empire stands and
    gods protect our fanes,
    Mankind with grateful hearts shall tell the
      story
How one most lowly born upon the parched
    Apulian plains
    First raised the native lyric muse to glory.

Assume, revered Melpomene, the proud es-
    tate I 've won,
    And, with thine own dear hand the meed
      supplying,
Bind thou about the forehead of thy cele-
    brated son
    The Delphic laurel-wreath of fame un-
      dying !

TO PHYLLIS

COME, Phyllis, I 've a cask of wine
    That fairly reeks with precious juices,
And in your tresses you shall twine
    The loveliest flowers this vale produces.

My cottage wears a gracious smile;
    The altar, decked in floral glory,
Yearns for the lamb which bleats the while
    As though it pined for honors gory.

Hither our neighbors nimbly fare,
    The boys agog, the maidens snickering;
And savory smells possess the air,
    As skyward kitchen flames are flickering.

You ask what means this grand display,
　　This festive throng and goodly diet?
Well, since you 're bound to have your way,
　　I don't mind telling, on the quiet.

'T is April 13, as you know,
　　A day and month devote to Venus,
Whereon was born, some years ago,
　　My very worthy friend, Mæcenas.

Nay, pay no heed to Telephus;
　　Your friends agree he does n't love you.
The way he flirts convinces us
　　He really is not worthy of you.

Aurora's son, unhappy lad!
　　You know the fate that overtook him?
And Pegasus a rider had,—
　　I say he *had,* before he shook him!

78

Hoc docet (as you must agree)
    'T is meet that Phyllis should discover
A wisdom in preferring me,
    And mittening every other lover.

So come, O Phyllis, last and best
    Of loves with which this heart 's been
        smitten,
Come, sing my jealous fears to rest,
    And let your songs be those *I 've* written.

TO PHYLLIS

II

SWEET Phyllis, I have here a jar of old
and precious wine,
The years which mark its coming from the
Alban hills are nine,
And in the garden parsley, too, for wreath-
ing garlands fair,
And ivy in profusion to bind up your shin-
ing hair.

Now smiles the house with silver; the
altar, laurel-bound,
Longs with the sacrificial blood of lambs to
drip around;
The company is hurrying, boys and maidens
with the rest;
The flames are flickering as they whirl the
dark smoke on their crest.

Yet you must know the joys to which you
    have been summoned here
To keep the Ides of April, to the sea-born
    Venus dear,—
Ah, festal day more sacred than my own
    fair day of birth,
Since from its dawn my loved Mæcenas
    counts his years of earth.

A rich and wanton girl has caught, as suited
    to her mind,
The Telephus whom you desire,—a youth
    not of your kind.
She holds him bound with pleasing chains,
    the fetters of her charms,—
Remember how scorched Phaëthon ambi-
    tious hopes alarms.

The winged Pegasus the rash Bellerophon
    has chafed,
To you a grave example for reflection has
    vouchsafed,—

Always to follow what is meet, and never
try to catch
That which is not allowed to you, an inap-
propriate match.

Come now, sweet Phyllis, of my loves the
last, and hence the best
(For nevermore shall other girls inflame this
manly breast);
Learn loving measures to rehearse as we
may stroll along,
And dismal cares shall fly away and vanish
at your song.

TO CHLOE

I

WHY do you shun me, Chloe, like the fawn,
That, fearful of the breezes and the wood,
Has sought her timorous mother since the
    dawn,
  And on the pathless mountain tops has
    stood?

Her trembling heart a thousand fears invites,
  Her sinking knees with nameless terrors
    shake,—
Whether the rustling leaf of spring affrights,
  Or the green lizards stir the slumbering
    brake.

I do not follow with a tigerish thought,
   Or with the fierce Gætulian lion's quest;
So, quickly leave your mother, as you
    ought,
   Full ripe to nestle on a husband's breast.

TO CHLOE

II

CHLOE, you shun me like a hind
   That, seeking vainly for her mother,
Hears danger in each breath of wind,
   And wildly darts this way and t' other;

Whether the breezes sway the wood
   Or lizards scuttle through the brambles,
She starts, and off, as though pursued,
   The foolish, frightened creature scrambles.

But, Chloe, you 're no infant thing
   That should esteem a man an ogre;
Let go your mother's apron-string,
   And pin your faith upon a toga!

A PARAPHRASE

HOW happens it, my cruel miss,
  You're always giving me the mitten?
You seem to have forgotten this:
  That you no longer are a kitten!

A woman that has reached the years
  Of that which people call discretion
Should put aside all childish fears
  And see in courtship no transgression.

A mother's solace may be sweet,
  But Hymen's tenderness is sweeter;
And though all virile love be meet,
  You'll find the poet's love is metre.

A PARAPHRASE, CIRCA 1715

SINCE Chloe is so monstrous fair,
　　With such an eye and such an air,
What wonder that the world complains
When she each am'rous suit disdains?

Close to her mother's side she clings,
And mocks the death her folly brings
To gentle swains that feel the smarts
Her eyes inflict upon their hearts.

Whilst thus the years of youth go by,
Shall Colin languish, Strephon die?
Nay, cruel nymph! come, choose a mate,
And choose him ere it be too late!

V

A PARAPHRASE, BY DR. I. W.

WHY, Mistress Chloe, do you bother
    With prattlings and with vain ado
Your worthy and industrious mother,
    Eschewing them that come to woo?

Oh, that the awful truth might quicken
    This stern conviction to your breast:
You are no longer now a chicken
    Too young to quit the parent nest.

So put aside your froward carriage,
    And fix your thoughts, whilst yet there's
        time,
Upon the righteousness of marriage
    With some such godly man as I'm.

A PARAPHRASE, BY CHAUCER

SYN that you, Chloe, to your moder
   sticken,
Maketh all ye yonge bacheloures full sicken;
Like as a lyttel deere you ben y-hiding
Whenas come lovers with theyre pityse
   chiding.
Sothly it ben faire to give up your moder
For to beare swete company with some oder;
Your moder ben well enow so farre shee
   goeth,
But that ben not farre enow, God knoweth;
Wherefore it ben sayed that foolysh ladyes
That marrye not shall leade an aype in Hadys;
But all that do with gode men wed full
   quicklye
When that they be on dead go to ye seints
   full sickerly.

TO MÆCENAS

THAN you, O valued friend of mine,
 A better patron *non est!*
Come, quaff my home-made Sabine wine,—
 You 'll find it poor but honest.

I put it up that famous day
 You patronized the ballet,
And the public cheered you such a way
 As shook your native valley.

Cæcuban and the Calean brand
 May elsewhere claim attention;
But *I* have none of these on hand,—
 For reasons I 'll not mention.

ENVOY

So, come! though favors I bestow
   Cannot be called extensive,
Who better than my friend should know
   That they 're at least expensive?

TO BARINE

IF for your oath broken, or word lightly
    spoken,
A plague comes, Barine, to grieve you;
If on tooth or on finger a black mark shall
    linger
Your beauty to mar, I'll believe you.

But no sooner, the fact is, you bind, as your
    tact is,
Your head with the vows of untruth,
Than you shine out more charming, and,
    what's more alarming,
You come forth beloved of our youth.

It is advantageous, but no less outrageous,
Your poor mother's ashes to cheat;
While the gods of creation and each con-
    stellation
You seem to regard as your meat.

Now Venus, I own it, is pleased to con-
    done it;
The good-natured nymphs merely smile;
And Cupid is merry,—'t is humorous,
    very,—
And sharpens his arrows the while.

Our boys you are making the slaves for
    your taking,
A new band is joined to the old;
While the horrified matrons your juvenile
    patrons
In vain would bring back to the fold.

The thrifty old fellows your loveliness mel-
 lows
Confess to a dread of your house;
But a more pressing duty, in view of your
 beauty,
Is the young wife's concern for her spouse.

THE RECONCILIATION

I

HE

WHEN you were mine, in auld lang
   syne,
   And when none else your charms might
      ogle,
I 'll not deny, fair nymph, that I
   Was happier than a heathen mogul.

SHE

Before *she* came, that rival flame
   (Had ever mater saucier filia ?),
In those good times, bepraised in rhymes,
   I was more famed than Mother Ilia.

HE

Chloe of Thrace!   With what a grace
　　Does she at song or harp employ her!
I 'd gladly die, if only I
　　Could live forever to enjoy her!

SHE

My Sybaris so noble is
　　That, by the gods, I love him madly!
That I might save him from the grave,
　　I 'd give my life, and give it gladly!

HE

What if *ma belle* from favor fell,
　　And I made up my mind to shake her;
Would Lydia then come back again,
　　And to her quondam love betake her?

SHE

My other beau should surely go,
　　And you alone should find me gracious;
For no one slings such odes and things
　　As does the lauriger Horatius!

THE RECONCILIATION

HORACE

WHILE favored by thy smiles no other
youth in amorous teasing
Around thy snowy neck his folding arms
was wont to fling;
As long as I remained your love, acceptable
and pleasing,
I lived a life of happiness beyond the Persian king.

LYDIA

While Lydia ranked Chloe in your unre-
served opinion,
And for no other cherished thou a brighter,
livelier flame,

I, Lydia, distinguished throughout the whole
    dominion,
    Surpassed the Roman Ilia in eminence of
      fame.

HORACE

'T is now the Thracian Chloe whose accom-
    plishments inthrall me,—
    So sweet in modulations, such a mistress
      of the lyre.
In truth the fates, however terrible, could
    not appall me;
    If they would spare her, sweet my soul, I
      gladly would expire.

LYDIA

And now the son of Ornytus, young Calais,
    inflames me
    With mutual, restless passion and an all-
      consuming fire;
And if the fates, however dread, would
    spare the youth who claims me,

Not only once would I face death, but
gladly twice expire.

HORACE

What if our early love returns to prove we
were mistaken
And bind with brazen yoke the twain, to
part, ah! nevermore?
What if the charming Chloe of the golden
locks be shaken
And slighted Lydia again glide through
the open door?

LYDIA

Though he is fairer than the star that shines
so far above you,
Thou lighter than a cork, more stormy
than the Adrian Sea,
Still should I long to live with you, to live
for you and love you,
And cheerfully see death's approach if
thou wert near to me.

THE ROASTING OF LYDIA

NO more your needed rest at night
   By ribald youth is troubled;
No more your windows, fastened tight,
   Yield to their knocks redoubled.

No longer you may hear them cry,
   "Why art thou, Lydia, lying
In heavy sleep till morn is nigh,
   While I, your love, am dying?"

Grown old and faded, you bewail
   The rake's insulting sally,
While round your home the Thracian gale
   Storms through the lonely alley.

What furious thoughts will fill your breast,
  What passions, fierce and tinglish
(Cannot be properly expressed
  In calm, reposeful English).

Learn this, and hold your carping tongue:
  Youth will be found rejoicing
In ivy green and myrtle young,
  The praise of fresh life voicing;

And not content to dedicate,
  With much protesting shiver,
The sapless leaves to winter's mate,
  Hebrus, the cold dark river.

TO GLYCERA

THE cruel mother of the Loves,
  And other Powers offended,
Have stirred my heart, where newly roves
  The passion that was ended.

'T is Glycera, to boldness prone,
  Whose radiant beauty fires me;
While fairer than the Parian stone
  Her dazzling face inspires me.

And on from Cyprus Venus speeds,
  Forbidding — ah! the pity —
The Scythian lays, the Parthian meeds,
  And such irrelevant ditty.

Here, boys, bring turf and vervain too;
   Have bowls of wine adjacent;
And ere our sacrifice is through
   She may be more complaisant.

TO LYDIA

I

WHEN, Lydia, you (once fond and
        true,
But now grown cold and supercilious)
Praise Telly's charms of neck and arms —
    Well, by the dog! it makes me bilious!

Then with despite my cheeks wax white,
    My doddering brain gets weak and giddy,
My eyes o'erflow with tears which show
    That passion melts my vitals, Liddy!

Deny, false jade, your escapade,
    And, lo! your wounded shoulders show
        it!
No manly spark left such a mark —
    Leastwise he surely was no poet!

With savage buss did Telephus
    Abraid your lips, so plump and mellow;
As you would save what Venus gave,
    I charge you shun that awkward fellow!

And now I say thrice happy they
    That call on Hymen to requite 'em;
For, though love cools, the wedded fools
    Must cleave till death doth disunite 'em.

TO LYDIA

II

WHEN praising Telephus you sing
His rosy neck and waxen arms,
Forgetful of the pangs that wring
This heart for my neglected charms,

Soft down my cheek the tear-drop flows,
My color comes and goes the while,
And my rebellious liver glows,
And fiercely swells with laboring bile.

Perchance yon silly, passionate youth,
Distempered by the fumes of wine,
Has marred your shoulder with his tooth,
Or scarred those rosy lips of thine.

106

Be warned; he cannot faithful prove,
Who, with the cruel kiss you prize,
Has hurt the little mouth I love,
Where Venus's own nectar lies.

Whom golden links unbroken bind,
Thrice happy — more than thrice are they;
And constant, both in heart and mind,
In love await the final day.

TO QUINTIUS HIRPINUS

TO Scythian and Cantabrian plots,
　　Pay them no heed, O Quintius!
　　　　So long as we
　　　　From care are free,
　Vexations cannot cinch us.

Unwrinkled youth and grace, forsooth,
　Speed hand in hand together;
　　　The songs we sing
　　　In time of spring
　Are hushed in wintry weather.

Why, even flow'rs change with the hours,
　And the moon has divers phases;
　　　And shall the mind
　　　Be racked to find
　A clew to Fortune's mazes?

Nay; 'neath this tree let you and me
  Woo Bacchus to caress us;
    We 're old, 't is true,
    But still we two
  Are thoroughbreds, God bless us!

While the wine gets cool in yonder pool,
  Let 's spruce up nice and tidy;
    Who knows, old boy,
    But we may decoy
  The fair but furtive Lyde?

She can execute on her ivory lute
  Sonatas full of passion,
    And she bangs her hair
    (Which is passing fair)
  In the good old Spartan fashion.

WINE, WOMEN, AND SONG

O VARUS mine,
    Plant thou the vine
Within this kindly soil of Tibur;
    Nor temporal woes,
    Nor spiritual, knows
The man who 's a discreet imbiber.
    For who doth croak
    Of being broke,
Or who of warfare, after drinking ?
    With bowl atween us,
    Of smiling Venus
And Bacchus shall we sing, I 'm thinking.

    Of symptoms fell
    Which brawls impel,
Historic data give us warning;
    The wretch who fights
    When full, of nights,

Is bound to have a head next morning.
> I do not scorn
> A friendly horn,
But noisy toots, I can't abide 'em!
> Your howling bat
> Is stale and flat
To one who knows, because he's tried 'em!

> The secrets of
> The life I love
(Companionship with girls and toddy)
> I would not drag
> With drunken brag
Into the ken of everybody;
> But in the shade
> Let some coy maid
With smilax wreathe my flagon's nozzle,
> Then all day long,
> With mirth and song,
Shall I enjoy a quiet sozzle!

111

AN ODE TO FORTUNE

O LADY FORTUNE! 't is to thee I
   call,
Dwelling at Antium, thou hast power to
   crown
The veriest clod with riches and renown,
   And change a triumph to a funeral.
The tillers of the soil and they that vex the
    seas,
Confessing thee supreme, on bended knees
   Invoke thee, all.

   Of Dacian tribes, of roving Scythian
    bands,
Of cities, nations, lawless tyrants red

With guiltless blood, art thou the haunting
    dread;
  Within thy path no human valor stands,
And, arbiter of empires, at thy frown
The sceptre, once supreme, slips surely
    down
  From kingly hands.

  Necessity precedes thee in thy way;
Hope fawns on thee, and Honor, too, is
    seen
Dancing attendance with obsequious mien;
  But with what coward and abject dismay
The faithless crowd and treacherous wan-
    tons fly
When once their jars of luscious wine run
    dry,—
  Such ingrates they!

  Fortune, I call on thee to bless
Our king,— our Cæsar girt for foreign wars!
Help him to heal these fratricidal scars

That speak degenerate shame and wicked-
    ness;
And forge anew our impious spears and
    swords,
Wherewith we may against barbarian
    hordes
  Our Past redress!

TO A JAR OF WINE

O GRACIOUS jar,— my friend, my twin,
　Born at the time when I was born,—
Whether tomfoolery you inspire
Or animate with love's desire,
　Or flame the soul with bitter scorn,
Or lull to sleep, O jar of mine!
　Come from your place this festal day;
　Corvinus hither wends his way,
And there 's demand for wine!

Corvinus is the sort of man
　Who dotes on tedious argument.
An advocate, his ponderous pate
　Is full of Blackstone and of Kent;
Yet not insensible is he,
O genial Massic flood! to thee.

Why, even Cato used to take
  A modest, surreptitious nip
At meal-times for his stomach's sake,
  Or to forefend la grippe.

How dost thou melt the stoniest hearts,
  And bare the cruel knave's design;
How through thy fascinating arts
  We discount Hope, O gracious wine!
And passing rich the poor man feels
As through his veins thy affluence steals.

Now, prithee, make us frisk and sing,
  And plot full many a naughty plot
With damsels fair — nor shall we care
  Whether school keeps or not!
And whilst thy charms hold out to burn
  We shall not deign to go to bed,
  But we shall paint creation red;
So, fill, sweet wine, this friend of mine,—
  My lawyer friend, as aforesaid.

TO POMPEIUS VARUS

POMPEY, what fortune gives you back
    To the friends and the gods who love
  you ?
Once more you stand in your native land,
  With your native sky above you.
Ah, side by side, in years agone,
    We 've faced tempestuous weather,
            And often quaffed
            The genial draught
  From the same canteen together.

When honor at Phillippi fell
  A prey to brutal passion,
I regret to say that my feet ran away
  In swift Iambic fashion.

117

You were no poet; soldier born,
  You stayed, nor did you wince then.
      Mercury came
        To my help, which same
  Has frequently saved me since then.

But now you 're back, let 's celebrate
  In the good old way and classic;
Come, let us lard our skins with nard,
  And bedew our souls with Massic!
With fillets of green parsley leaves
  Our foreheads shall be done up;
        And with song shall we
          Protract our spree
  Until the morrow's sun-up.

THE POET'S METAMORPHOSIS

MÆCENAS, I propose to fly
    To realms beyond these human
  portals;
No common things shall be my wings,
  But such as sprout upon immortals.

Of lowly birth, once shed of earth,
  Your Horace, precious (so you 've told
    him),
Shall soar away; no tomb of clay
  Nor Stygian prison-house shall hold him.

Upon my skin feathers begin
  To warn the songster of his fleeting;
But never mind, I leave behind
  Songs all the world shall keep repeating.

Lo! Boston girls, with corkscrew curls,
  And husky westerns, wild and woolly,
And southern climes shall vaunt my rhymes,
  And all profess to know me fully.

Methinks the West shall know me best,
  And therefore hold my memory dearer;
For by that lake a bard shall make
  My subtle, hidden meanings clearer.

So cherished, I shall never die;
  Pray, therefore, spare your dolesome
    praises,
Your elegies, and plaintive cries,
  For I shall fertilize no daisies!

TO VENUS

VENUS, dear Cnidian-Paphian queen!
　　Desert that Cyprus way off yonder,
And fare you hence, where with incense
　　My Glycera would have you fonder;
And to your joy bring hence your boy,
　　The Graces with unbelted laughter,
The Nymphs, and Youth,— then, then, in
　　　sooth,
　　Should Mercury come tagging after.

IN THE SPRINGTIME

I

'T IS spring! The boats bound to the sea;
   The breezes, loitering kindly over
The fields, again bring herds and men
   The grateful cheer of honeyed clover.

Now Venus hither leads her train;
   The Nymphs and Graces join in orgies;
The moon is bright, and by her light
   Old Vulcan kindles up his forges.

Bind myrtle now about your brow,
   And weave fair flowers in maiden tresses;
Appease god Pan, who, kind to man,
   Our fleeting life with affluence blesses;

But let the changing seasons mind us,
 That Death 's the certain doom of mor-
  tals, —
Grim Death, who waits at humble gates,
 And likewise stalks through kingly por-
  tals.

Soon, Sestius, shall Plutonian shades
 Enfold you with their hideous seemings;
Then love and mirth and joys of earth
 Shall fade away like fevered dreamings.

IN THE SPRINGTIME

II

THE western breeze is springing up, the
    ships are in the bay,
And spring has brought a happy change as
    winter melts away.
No more in stall or fire the herd or plowman
    finds delight;
No longer with the biting frosts the open
    fields are white.

Our Lady of Cythera now prepares to lead
    the dance,
While from above the kindly moon gives an
    approving glance;

The Nymphs and comely Graces join with
    Venus and the choir,
And Vulcan's glowing fancy lightly turns to
    thoughts of fire.

Now it is time with myrtle green to crown
    the shining pate,
And with the early blossoms of the spring to
    decorate;
To sacrifice to Faunus, on whose favor we
    rely,
A sprightly lamb, mayhap a kid, as he may
    specify.

Impartially the feet of Death at huts and
    castles strike;
The influenza carries off the rich and poor
    alike.
O Sestius, though blessed you are beyond
    the common run,
Life is too short to cherish e'en a distant hope
    begun.

The Shades and Pluto's mansion follow hard
    upon the grip.
Once there you cannot throw the dice, nor
    taste the wine you sip;
Nor look on blooming Lycidas, whose beauty
    you commend,
To whom the girls will presently their cour-
    tesies extend.

TO A BULLY.

YOU, blatant coward that you are,
  Upon the helpless vent your spite.
Suppose you ply your trade on me;
Come, monkey with this bard, and see
  How I 'll repay your bark with bite!

Ay, snarl just once at me, you brute!
  And I shall hound you far and wide,
As fiercely as through drifted snow
The shepherd dog pursues what foe
  Skulks on the Spartan mountain-side.

The chip is on my shoulder — see?
  But touch it and I 'll raise your fur;
I 'm full of business, so beware!
For, though I 'm loaded up for bear,
  I 'm quite as like to kill a cur!

127

TO MOTHER VENUS

O MOTHER VENUS, quit, I pray,
　　Your violent assailing!
The arts, forsooth, that fired my youth
　　At last are unavailing;
My blood runs cold, I 'm getting old,
　　And all my powers are failing.

Speed thou upon thy white swans' wings,
　　And elsewhere deign to mellow
With thy soft arts the anguished hearts
　　Of swains that writhe and bellow;
And right away seek out, I pray,
　　Young Paullus,— he 's your fellow!

128

You 'll find young Paullus passing fair,
   Modest, refined, and tony;
Go, now, incite the favored wight!
   With Venus for a crony
He 'll outshine all at feast and ball
   And conversazione!

Then shall that godlike nose of thine
   With perfumes be requited,
And then shall prance in Salian dance
   The girls and boys delighted,
And while the lute blends with the flute
   Shall tender loves be plighted.

But as for me, as you can see,
   I 'm getting old and spiteful.
I have no mind to female kind,
   That once I deemed delightful;
No more brim up the festive cup
   That sent me home at night full.

Why do I falter in my speech,
   O cruel Ligurine?
Why do I chase from place to place
   In weather wet and shiny?
Why down my nose forever flows
   The tear that 's cold and briny?

TO LYDIA

TELL me, Lydia, tell me why,
    By the gods that dwell above,
Sybaris makes haste to die
    Through your cruel, fatal love.

Now he hates the sunny plain;
    Once he loved its dust and heat.
Now no more he leads the train
    Of his peers on coursers fleet.

Now he dreads the Tiber's touch,
    And avoids the wrestling-rings,—
He who formerly was such
    An expert with quoits and things.

131

Come, now, Mistress Lydia, say
    Why your Sybaris lies hid,
Why he shuns the martial play,
    As we 're told Achilles did.

TO NEOBULE

A SORRY life, forsooth, these wretched
    girls are undergoing,
Restrained from draughts of pleasant wine,
    from loving favors showing,
For fear an uncle's tongue a reprimand will
    be bestowing!

Sweet Cytherea's winged boy deprives you
    of your spinning,
And Hebrus, Neobule, his sad havoc is be-
    ginning,
Just as Minerva thriftily gets ready for an
    inning.

133

Who could resist this gallant youth, as Tiber's waves he breasted,
Or when the palm of riding from Bellerophon he wrested,
Or when with fists and feet the sluggers
easily he bested?

He shot the fleeing stags with regularity
surprising;
The way he intercepted boars was quite beyond surmising,—
No wonder that your thoughts this youth
has been monopolizing!

So I repeat that with these maids fate is
unkindly dealing,
Who never can in love's affair give license
to their feeling,
Or share those sweet emotions when a
gentle jag is stealing.

AT THE BALL GAME

WHAT gods or heroes, whose brave
deeds none can dispute,
Will you record, O Clio, on the harp and
flute?
What lofty names shall sportive Echo grant
a place
On Pindus' crown or Helicon's cool, shadowy
space?

Sing not, my Orpheus, sweeping oft the
tuneful strings,
Of gliding streams and nimble winds and
such poor things;
But lend your measures to a theme of noble
thought,
And crown with laurel these great heroes,
as you ought.

135

Now steps Ryanus forth at call of furious
    Mars,

And from his oaken staff the sphere speeds
    to the stars;

And now he gains the tertiary goal, and
    turns,

While whiskered balls play round the timid
    staff of Burns.

Lo! from the tribunes on the bleachers comes
    a shout,

Beseeching bold Ansonius to line 'em out;

And as Apollo's flying chariot cleaves the
    sky,

So stanch Ansonius lifts the frightened ball on
    high.

Like roar of ocean beating on the Cretan
    cliff,

The strong Komiske gives the panting sphere
    a biff;

And from the tribunes rise loud murmurs
    everywhere,
When twice and thrice Mikellius beats the
    mocking air.

And as Achilles' fleet the Trojan waters
    sweeps,
So horror sways the throng,—Pfefferius
    sleeps!
And stalwart Konnor, though by Mercury
    inspired,
The Equus Carolus defies, and is retired.

So waxes fierce the strife between these god-
    like men;
And as the hero's fame grows by Virgilian
    pen,
So let Clarksonius Maximus be raised to
    heights
As far above the moon as moon o'er lesser
    lights.

But as for me, the ivy leaf is my reward,
If you a place among the lyric bards accord;
With crest exalted, and O "People," with
    delight,
I 'll proudly strike the stars, and so be out
    of sight.

EPILOGUE

THE day is done; and, lo! the shades
    Melt 'neath Diana's mellow grace.
Hark, how those deep, designing maids
    Feign terror in this sylvan place!
Come, friends, it 's time that we should go;
We 're honest married folk, you know.

Was not the wine delicious cool
    Whose sweetness Pyrrha's smile en-
      hanced?
And by that clear Bandusian pool
    How gayly Chloe sung and danced!
And Lydia Dic,— aha, methinks
You 'll not forget the saucy minx!

But, oh, the echoes of those songs
   That soothed our cares and lulled our
     hearts!
Not to that age nor this belongs
   The glory of what heaven-born arts
Speak with the old distinctive charm
From yonder humble Sabine farm!

The day is done. Now off to bed,
   Lest by some rural ruse surprised,
And by those artful girls misled,
   You two be sadly compromised.
You go; perhaps *I* 'd better stay
To shoo the giddy things away!

But sometime we shall meet again
   Beside Digentia, cool and clear,—
You and we twain, old friend; and then
   We 'll have our fill of pagan cheer.
Then, could old Horace join us three,
How proud and happy he would be!

Or if we part to meet no more
   This side the misty Stygian Sea,
Be sure of this: on yonder shore
   Sweet cheer awaiteth such as we;
A Sabine pagan's heaven, O friend,—
The fellowship that knows no end!

              E. F.